This book is from:

_____

To you

_____

Illustrations by Kenn Yapsangco

Copyright © 2013 by Meghann Timms

All rights reserved. No part of this book may be reproduced or transmitted in any form or by any means, electronic or mechanical, including photocopying, recording, or by any information storage and retrieval system, without permission in writing from the copyright owner.

This is a work of fiction. Names, characters, places and incidents either are the product of the author's imagination or are used fictitiously, and any resemblance to any actual persons, living or dead, events, or locales is entirely coincidental.

They truly are a sight to see,
The Yorkies! Not one...not two...yes, three!
Running and playing, they have so much fun.
The Yorkies brighten your room like the sun.

Beso-
He's fast, and cute, and coy.
What's that in his mouth?
His favorite toy!

Bon Bon-
named after
the chocolate treat,
Why, you might ask?
Well, she's just so sweet!

Buster-
Now, he is the smallest of all.
But...guess what?
HE doesn't think so...no, not at all!

One grabs a chew and the others give chase,
As if they were really running a race.
Those cute lil' Yorkies go-go-go,
Their owners *love* to watch the show.

The pups go 'round and 'round the room,
You can hear their motors-*screech*!
Vroom, vroom!
Faster and faster they fly through the air,
You would think the Yorkies didn't like to share.

When they hear keys jingling,
And the shuffling of feet,
The Yorkies stop *everything*,
for a ride in the backseat.

Watching objects whiz by
as they pass,
Paws and wet noses pressed up
against glass.
Cuddly, furry, cute as can be,
The Yorkies go *everywhere* with you
and me.

Awaiting the drive-up window,
And tasty, cool treats.
Tails start awaggin',
Oh my, what good eats!

Later, back home, it is time to rest, the Yorkies head to the place they love best.
Whoosh! Jumping into
a nice, cozy lap,
drowsy and more than ready to nap.

Resting those bodies,
they fall fast asleep.
The Yorkies-oh, such
a schedule to keep.
But-shh!-don't be fooled, they
won't sleep all day.
Soon they'll awaken...and be ready
to play.

www.ingramcontent.com/pod-product-compliance
Lightning Source LLC
LaVergne TN
LVHW072114060526
838200LV00061B/4890